# THE
# BEE'S
# KNEES

# THE BEE'S KNEES

JAMES MORRISSEY

Interviews by LORNA SIGGINS

CURRACH
BOOKS

First published in 2020 by

 CURRACHBOOKS

23 Merrion Square North, Dublin 2

www.currachbooks.com

ISBN: 978-1-78218-918-3

Cover and book design by Alba Esteban | Currach Books

Printed by L&C Poland

*How doth the little busy bee*
*Improve each shining hour*
*And gather honey all day*
*From every opening flower*

– Isaac Watts, *Against Idleness.*

# CONTENTS

# INTRODUCTION

One of the questions most frequently asked of beekeepers is: "Why do bees matter?"

The answer is very simple: Most crops in the world depend primarily on pollinators. Bees pollinate by 'carrying' pollen from flower to flower, a vital element in the reproductive cycle of certain plants that produce three out of every four crops in the world including almonds, apples, grapes, blackberries, strawberries, coffee, tomatoes and beans. Pollinator-dependent foods are vital to nutrition and healthy diets. Among the other pollinators are butterflies, hummingbirds, beetles and ants.

Bees are under enormous threat in the world. According to the Food and Agriculture Organisation of the United Nations extinction rates of pollinators are 100 to 1,000 times higher than normal due to human impacts. These include increased use of pesticides and pests, and diseases triggering reduced resistance of bee colonies.

Global warming, floods, and droughts are altering flowering routines which is impacting on bee behaviour and... pollination.

Ireland has had a long association with beekeeping. In the 7th Century a set of laws relating to beekeeping were compiled under Brehon law. Administered by the Brehons, the laws were particularly progressive and ranged from recognising equal rights between genders to dealing with wrongdoing by restitution rather than punishment.

Beekeeping in Ireland is on the increase but not without the same global challenges of disease.

The native Irish honeybee (also native to the UK and Northern Europe) *Apis mellifera mellifera* (A.m.m.) has, over thousands of years, adapted to the Irish climate.

The Native Irish Honey Bee Society (NIHBS) was established in 2012 to conserve the native bee.

"Bees have a vital role in Irish agriculture and through their essential pollination services, they contribute significantly to our food production," the Society has stated.

The importation of foreign subspecies and hybrids lead to mongrelisation and recently the Society called for a ban on imports.

Anyone who has tasted pure Irish honey knows that it is one of our finest products.

I first encountered honeybees when my family acquired two swarms to take up residence in hives in the garden of our family home in Kiltimagh, Co. Mayo.

Beekeeping in the west of Ireland got a renewed boost in the late 19th Century when the Congested Districts Board encouraged it as a source of income post Famine.

Years later I came across *Instructions for Managing Bees* - Drawn up and published by order of the Dublin Society, 1733.

Then some years ago I learned that a neighbour in Connemara, Gerard Coyne, was an avid beekeeper and I asked if he would tutor me. I learned from the best. Gerard has been a wonderful mentor to so many new beekeepers all over Ireland and an inspirational leader in promoting the protection of the native Irish honeybee. He follows in the illustrious footsteps of Turlough O'Bryen and Dan Deasy.

Peter, my brother, has also been a guiding light: always willing to calmly impart his extensive knowledge when I believe I have angered a hive by some incorrect procedure... again.

When I suggested this book to Garry O'Sullivan of Currach Books less than a year ago, his response was instantly positive: "When will you have it written?" And his recommendation to invite Lorna Siggins, one of Ireland's finest journalists, to conduct the interviews, was enlightened.

Alba Esteban, Currach's designer, immersed herself in this book, constantly pushing the design parameters.

This book has been a thoroughly enjoyable project, primarily because it has been a lesson in self-learning about an aspect of nature in the world we co-share.

*James Morrissey*

Beekeeper Gerard Coyne takes a closer look during a hive inspection.

# CHAPTER 1

# BEES ACROSS HISTORY

Gathering Honey, Tomb of Rekhmire, circa 1479 – 1425 B.C. Metropolitan Museum of Art. Source: Wikimedia Commons.

Bees have been around for a very long time. A bee found preserved in amber in Myanmar (formerly Burma) is estimated to date back to the Cretaceous period, some 100 million years ago.

It is believed that honey-storing bees made their nests in holes in the ground and also in trees during the Miocene over 10 million years ago.

Paintings on rocks in the Cave of the Spider, close to Bicorp in Valencia, Spain, are among the earliest visual records of beekeeping. According to *The History of Beekeeping* (by Destrier) the drawings are Late Palaeolithic or Mesolithic period: "Two honey collectors hang by what appear to be creepers or possibly a ladder of creepers on rope. One carried a vessel slung over his back, the other, a woman, investigates the bees' nest with her right arm, while she holds a container for the comb in her left hand. A few bees are flying around; but she seems to be quietening the bees with smoke."

Egyptians used honey for everything from a sweetening ingredient to preserving corpses.

For as far back as 3,000 BC Egyptians kept records of beekeeping – records were found in the sun temple built near Cairo in 2400BC. Bees were ferried south on the Nile to lands where flowers were more abundant, thus ensuring a richer harvest. Indeed, beekeeping was carried out most intensely in Lower Egypt and one of the pharaoh's titles was Bee King. The bee was also selected as the symbol for the country.

In a 4th Century papyrus, there is a description of the hive:

> *"One does not build a royal palace for the honey bee. A hive of dung is better than a hive of stone...the house of the bee is effectively an arrangement of combs, a place suitable for storing honey... it is more pleasant for the bees beneath the combs."* – Eva Crane, *The World History of Beekeeping and Honey Hunting*, 1999.

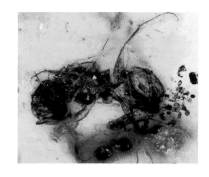

*Melittosphex burmensis*, one of the two oldest-known species of bees, was found in an amber mine in the Hukawng Valley, Kachin state, northern Myanmar (Burma) in 2006.

Bust of Aristotle by Lysippos, c. 330 BC.

The oldest sacred book in India, *The Rig-Veda*, (between 3,000 and 2,000 BC) includes many references to bees and honey. A collection of some 1,000 hymns, the Rig is the oldest of four Vedas (Sama, Vajur, Athara and Rig), which focus on the mythology of the Hindu gods and is recognised as the foundation of the Hindu religion. The written form was recorded in 300BC.

The Greeks used honey for various purposes from food consumption to medicine. Cheeses were served with honey and the combination of both in cheesecakes was described by Euripedes as "steeped most thoroughly in the rich honey of the golden bee."

During the 'Golden Age' in Greece (600-140BC) bees and honey were much studied. For example, the *Illiad* and the *Odyssy*, refer to honey.

But it was Aristotle who has provided us with a detailed account of bees from his *History of Animals*, a massive tome of ten books.

Aristotle, (384-322 BC) the Greek philosopher who was taught by Plato, lived during the time of Alexander the Great. He was chosen by Philip, King of Macedon, to educate Alexander, his son. He is credited with pioneering work in natural science, metaphysics, logic, ethics, politics and literary criticism.

Aristotle's *History of Animals* is fascinating in that Man was perceived as the perfect animal with the capacity to think, speak and to reason. Aristotle writes about bees – not as a beekeeper, because he wasn't, but from his observations and contact with those who had experience with bees and honey.

He was not sure of the sex of the 'bee in charge' in the hive but explained: "Their size is doubler that of the worker bees... by some they are called the mother bee... as if they were parents to the rest... and they argue, that unless the ruler is present, drones are only produced and no bees... others affirm that they have sexual intercourse and that drones are males and the bees females..."

Virgil, the ancient Roman poet (70 BC – 19 BC), deals extensively with bee-keeping in *Georgics: Book IV* and extols the reader to learn about "the celestial gift of honey from the air."

He identifies their highly-structured summer planning for winter supplies:

*"For some supervise the gathering of food, and work*
*in the fields to an agreed rule: some, walled in their homes,*
*lay the first foundations of the comb, with drops of gum*
*taken from narcissi, and sticky glue from tree-bark,*
*then hang the clinging wax: others lead the mature young,*
*their nation's hope, other pack purest honey together,*
*and swell the cells with liquid nectar:*
*there are those whose lot it is to guard the gates."*

An early theory was that when bees leave the hive they generally fly into the wind in search of pollen. Why? So that their homeward cargo-laden journey would be less onerous with the wind at their backs.

Israel has been referred to as "the land of milk and honey" in the Old Testament of the Bible, while mead was referred to as "nectar of the gods."

There are many references to honey in the Bible:

Ezekiel 20:6
*"On that day I swore to them*
*that I would bring them out*
*of the land of Egypt into a*
*land that I had searched*
*out for them, a land*
*flowing with milk and honey,*
*the most glorious of lands."*

Song of Solomon 4:11
*"Your lips drip nectar, my bride,*
*honey and milk are under your*
*tongue, the fragrance of your garments is like*
*the fragrance of Lebanon."*

## KEY FACTS ABOUT BEES

Honey bees live together in hives, also known as colonies.

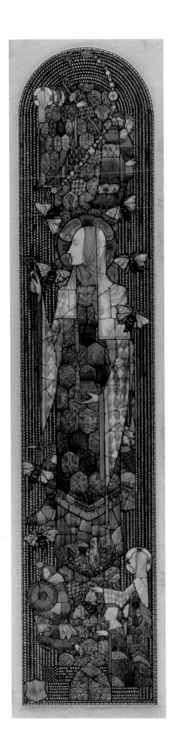

Exodus 16:31

*"Now the house of Israel called its name manna. It was like coriander seed, white, and the taste of it was like wafers made of honey."*

Honey was widely used in burial and funeral ceremonies among many nationalities including Egyptians, Greeks, Romans, Chinese and Hindus. It was frequently placed beside the body of the deceased.

To this day African tribes use honey in burial rituals.

It has been suggested that honey represented the sweetness of death as compared with the bitterness of life.

◄ Stained glass artist and illustrator Harry Clarke (1889-1931) drew this design for a stained glass window featuring Saint Gobnait of Ballyvourney, a sixth-century patron saint of beekeepers. The window is installed on the south side of the nave of Honan Chapel, Cork, and is one of a series of windows Clarke designed for Honan Chapel.

Bee at the entrance to the 'bee bed' which keeper David Geoghegan designed and built at his home overlooking Lough Corrib in Co. Galway.

# CHAPTER 2

# BEE JUDGEMENTS

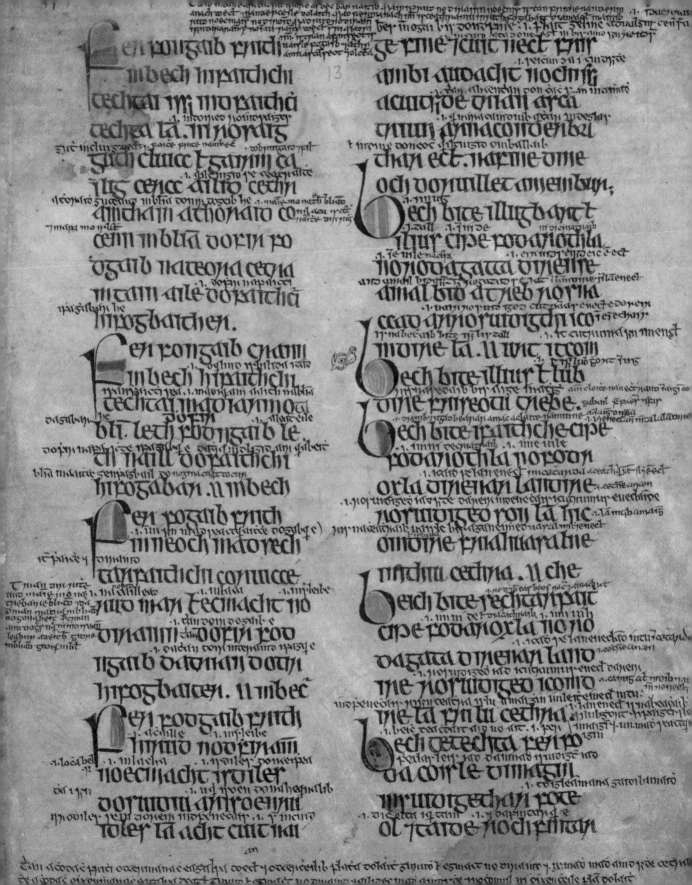

Ireland had its own legal system going back to Celtic times and it survived until King James I of England, by Proclamation in 1603, replaced it with English common law.

The Brehon Laws were very progressive. Divorce was recognised as were equal rights between male and female. They were verbally passed down from generation to generation until they were written down in the 7th Century.

Judges were called Brehons and hence the name given to the system of law. Brehons succeeded the Celtic druids and their role was more of arbitrator than judge. Elevation to the position of Brehon followed a period of study and training. They were, by their very nature, extremely powerful and influential as disputes and other contentious matters were adjudicated by them.

Brehons belonged to the privileged classes and enjoyed the goodwill and generosity of local chiefs. The "laws" were complicated, and interpretations were many and varied. But getting it wrong carried with it the risk of having to pay damages or forfeiture of a fee.

In the earliest years of the Brehon Laws it was thought that the Brehons had some form of divine power maintaining a watching brief over their judgements and decisions. Judgements regarded as unfair were subject to punishment from a higher power.

"When the Brehons deviated from the truth, there appeared blotches on their cheeks." It was said that the Great Brehon, Morann, son of Carberry Kinncat (King of Ireland in the 1st Century) wore a special collar around his neck. When he delivered a false or incorrect judgement the collar got tighter... and loosened when a correct decision was handed down."

Sir John Davies, Attorney General in Ireland during the reign of King James I was impressed by the adherence of the Irish people to the laws of their country: "For there is no nation of people under the

## KEY FACTS ABOUT HONEY

An average one pound jar of honey requires bees to fly the equivalent of over two times around the world.

◄ *Opposite:* Page 25 of the Senchus Mór, 14th Century collection of law tracts, detailing here the Bechbretha, the early Irish laws of bee keeping.

sun that doth love all equally and indifferent (i.e. impartial) justice better than the Irish; or will rest better satisfied with the execution thereof, although it bee (sic) against themselves: so as they may have the protection and benefit of the law, when upon just cause they do desire it."

Wrongdoing was dealt with more by restitution than punishment.

The Brehon Laws also had a section relating to bees and beekeeping. Bechbretha, "bee judgements" are probably the oldest and only set of such legal rulings in the world. This unique document is the oldest Irish legal manuscript and is preserved in the Library of Trinity College Dublin.

These bee judgements are explained in detail in Bechbretha, *Early Irish Law Series Volume 1*, edited by Thomas Charles-Edwards and Fergus Kelly.

Bees, we are told, are not to be compared to animals such as cows and pigs.

The challenge for the Brehon is to achieve a balance between allowing a new hive to become established and to bring some return to the beekeeper and, on the other hand, to the neighbour's time to get their own hive set up from the swarms emanating from the first hive. Hence the period of three years immunity.

> *"The proposed solution has much to recommend it: it gives the owner his temporary immunity and yet gives his neighbours their swarms. Once the neighbours have received their swarms they too will enjoy a period of immunity after which everyone will be on the same footing. The solution protects the first bee-keeper and yet spreads the asset throughout the group of neighbours."*

And just as farm animals trespass so do bees and this had to be dealt with in the bee judgements.

The ruling was based on a judgement covering the fruit of a tree which had branches overhanging into a neighbour's land. This is the

Honey is the only
food from insects that
humans consume.

origin of the three years of immunity – the neighbour on whose land the fruit falls is entitled to half of it for the first three years and all of it in the fourth year.

And so with the honey from bees who have attached themselves to the over-hanging branch: "If it is bees which have settled there, they divide the produce in half between them for three years, but it is to (the owner of) the land from which it (tree) grows that the source of the produce belongs (i.e. the bees)."

The authors of the bee judgements were very insightful in their directions for dealing with issues and disputes, suggesting also that beekeeping was an important aspect of rural life in Ireland, as a source of income as well as a food sweetener.

For example, a man attacked by bees while in the act of robbing them of their produce simply suffered the consequences devoid of sympathy. But the person attacked while going about their business is wronged "for this is an injury which entails his sufficiency of honey (for the man who is stung there)."

However, he must not kill the offending insect. "with an oath from him that he did not kill the bee which stung him; for if it is killed it compensates for its offence as in every other case".

And in the event of an eye blinded by a bee sting the settlement is for the casting of lots on all the hives in that location and whichever hive is selected is forfeited as the fine. (This apparently was the first judgement following an eye sting suffered by 'Congal the One-Eyed.')

Then there is the scenario where a person tracks a swarm of bees to land owned by 'a dignitary'. "Tracked bees which settle in the branches of a dignitary [...] the dignitary is entitled to a third of the produce for a year, the other two thirds (go) to the man who tracks them and who is their original owner, but it is he who looks after them, for the third which goes to the dignitary is a gratuity."

And the man lucky enough to follow a swarm (that is not his) to the place there the bees settle is entitled to a third of the produce (the other two thirds go to the owner of the land where they settle and the owner of the hive from which they departed).

# CHAPTER 3

# IRISH BEEKEEPERS ASSOCIATION

I n 1731 the Dublin Society was set up by a group of men from Trinity College to promote the development of science, agriculture and the arts.

Two years later it published a detailed paper, *Instructions for Managing Bees*, by an unnamed author: "It is proposed in the following Paper to give some short Account of Bees; to lay down Instructions for the due Management of them, in such manners as to procure with Ease and Plenty, the useful Produce of Honey and Wax which they afford; and then to consider the great Profit that arises from this Branch of Husbandry, as an Encouragement of the Farmer to bestow some pains upon what will afford him so plentiful a Recompence."

Those solely interested in keeping bees without proper care and attention were duly admonished: "Most people when by Exchange, Gift or otherwise, they have got an Hive of Bees (for there is a ridiculous Superstition, that if they are bought, they won't thrive) leave them carefully upon a Stool, in any Situation: If they happen to thrive, they are well please'd with the Produce, but never mind whether they do or no, till they come to enquire what they can get from them; but if thro' Neglect they miscarry, if they be plundered by Vermin or other Bees, or if they perish for want of Food, they then impute the Miscarriage to the wetness and the windiness of the Season, which ought rather to be charged to their own Neglect."

The monetary benefits were also highlighted at about five shillings per hive: "That this Value of an Hive is much within compass, will appear from hence, that a good Hive when taken, will yield from Eight to Ten Quarts of Honey, and from One Pound and half to Two Pounds of Wax; the Honey being worth 9d per quart at a medium, and the Wax 14d. Per Pound, the Value of an Hive will be eight Shillings and six Pence."

And then there was the making of Mead: "Some People choose in making this Wine, to mix Brandy, Spices and other Substances there-

Cover of the *Reprinted Papers on Bee Husbandry*, published by the Royal Dublin Society in 1980.

◄ *Opposite*: Beekeepers Pat Collins, (left) and Ger Ryan, Chairman tending to their beehives at St Mary's Parish Men's Shed on Nicholas Street, in the historic King's Island area of Limerick City.

▲ Famine Memorial, Doo Lough, County Mayo. A simple cross marks the location in Doo Lough where many, trying to escape the famine, perished having not found the support they sought.

with in the brewing, which depend on the Fancy of the Owners, and may sometimes be useful, but I believe oftner do Harm than Good."

The writer refers to a gentleman of his acquaintance who has provided members of the Dublin Society with recipes for two kinds of mead: "He makes two sorts, the smaller he drinks at Meals, the stronger at other Times, and can with Pleasure drink a Bottle of it."

Over a century after this document was published Ireland suffered the Great Famine which claimed the lives of over one million people and resulted in another one million emigrating.

By the late 19th Century the plight of the Irish people had improved little. One observer noted: "I have seen a half-naked child of four to five years lying asleep before the turf fire, with his head on a rough block of wood, while the cow stood over him, as if watching and guarding the child."

Most of the inhabitants of the West of Ireland eked out a meagre existence in conditions proximate to pathetic. Homes were akin to hovels as parents and offspring shared cramped accommodation with farm animals. Incomes were paltry – ranging from less than £10 per year to just under £50 for families.

Interest in beekeeping was in evidence around Ireland and it was this that prompted the establishing of the Irish Beekeepers Association in 1881 in the Royal Dublin Society (previously the Dublin Society).

In 1890 Arthur Balfour, Chief Secretary for Ireland, undertook a tour of the 'congested districts' of the west of Ireland. These were areas that were regarded as exceptionally poor and undeveloped.

He later wrote: "The general impression left upon the casual traveler is that you are dealing with a population not congested in the sense of being crowded, but congested by not being able to draw from their holdings a safe and sufficient livelihood for themselves and their children whose condition trembles constantly on the verge of want, and when the potato crop fails, goes over that margin and becomes one of extreme and even dangerous destitution."

The visit resulted in the setting up of The Congested Districts Board established by the Land Act of 1891 to provide assistance to impoverished areas where "in a good year (the people) are little more than free from the dread of hunger."

The areas consisted of counties Donegal, Leitrim, Sligo, Roscommon, Mayo, Galway, Clare, Kerry and West Cork.

Assistance was given to support improvements in housing, livestock, cottage industries and fishing.

Subsequently, a team of inspectors traversed this part of Ireland to undertake a survey for the purposes of finding out the exact living conditions and identifying what projects could create employment and derive benefit from land and sea.

Many initiatives were launched including the building of new homes, improving of animal husbandry, achieving higher returns from growing vegetables and other crops, fishing and beekeeping.

Arthur Balfour, chief secretary for Ireland from 1887 to 1891.

CHAPTER 4

# THE BEE MAN OF COUNTY CLARE

# THURLES & DISTRICT BEEKEEPERS' ASSOCIATION.

## A PUBLIC
# DEMONSTRATION IN BEEKEEPING,

WILL BE GIVEN BY

## Mr. T. B. O'BRYEN,

### THE DEPARTMENTS' EXPERT IN BEEKEEPING,

— AT —

# MR. C. J. MOLLOY'S,

### Beakstown Mills, Holycross,

— ON —

# Tuesday, July 25th, 1911.

## At ONE O'CLOCK.

All interested in Beekeeping are requested to attend.
In order to follow closely the Course of Instruction,
and to avoid being stung by Bees, it is advisable to
bring a Veil.

*Teas will be served on the Grounds at Sixpence each.*

## PROGRAMME.

I. Short Address by Mr. O'Bryen, stating the Advantages of Beekeeping
   Associations.

II. Enrolling New Members, taking Subscriptions, etc.

III. The advantages of Modern Hives over the Cheaper and Old Fashioned
    Classes.

IV. Discussion and Demonstration on the Making of Artificial Swarms, and the
    Subduing of Bees.

V. The Filling and Removing of Crates, and Working a Modern Hive to
   Advantage.

VI. Discussion and Demonstration on the Preparing of Sections for Market.

VII. Extracting and its Advantages.

VIII. Questions from Members, which are freely invited, will be discussed.

*The Heating of Hives, Preparing Honey for Market, Brood Extending,
How to Keep Apiaries free from Disease, and many other subjects of
interest to Beekeepers will be dealt with.*

NOTE.—All Members of the above Association are requested to attend, and also to use
their influence with the Beekeepers in their several districts to be present, and
take advantage of the above Demonstration, which is certain to prove of the
greatest value and interest.

GLEESON & SON, PRINTERS, NENAGH.

"It has been estimated that one hive may in a good year produce as much profit as a pig," Francis Sheridan, chief clerk at the Congested Districts Board (CDB) wrote in 1915.

Beekeeping was given special attention, he said, "owing to its particular suitability as a cottage industry, and the capital required is so very little while a very high level percentage of profit is obtainable."

But the Board needed someone who would travel around Ireland assisting existing beekeepers to achieve higher levels of production with improved methods and better equipment. The Irish Beekeepers Association had among its members Turlough O'Bryen, a native of Louth and now living in Co. Clare. He had started beekeeping in the mid-1870s, initially without much success.

O'Bryen joined the Board in 1893 as an instructor.

"With modest funding... Turlough traveled on his push bike... he was frequently to be seen in all sorts of weather on his bicycle, on which he used to carry a great deal of frames...and other requisites, delivering them to beekeepers as he went". Eva Crane, the International Bee Research Association, later wrote.

> "He took his two bicycles with him on the GWR (Great Western Railway) to the station nearest his working area for that week, leaving one at the station, he loaded up the pannier of the other and proceeded to his first engagement...supplies could be delivered to the various hotels that he had planned to stay at and where he resorted to at the end of the day to compile his reports."

Book cover of *The Bee Man of County Clare* by James K. Watson, 1995.

◄*Opposite:* Poster promoting beekeeping classes by Turlough O'Bryen at Holycross, Co. Tipperary in 1911. Image from book *The Bee Man of County Clare* by James K. Watson, 1995.

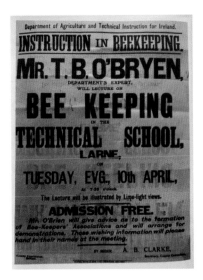

Poster promoting beekeeping classes by Turlough O'Bryen. Image from book *The Bee Man of County Clare* by James K. Watson, 1995.

**KEY FACTS
ABOUT HONEY**

A pound of honey is produced from bees collecting 10 pounds of nectar from flowers.

When he joined the CDB he moved to Kingstown (Dun Laoghaire):

*"Commencing the week's work, he travelled by train from Kingstown Station into town on Mondays, went to the Irish Agricultural Organisation Society in Thomas Street, Dublin, where he ordered his supplies of hives, wax, frames and sections to be delivered to whatever railway station he was working from."*
– 'The Bee Man of County Clare – Turlough Butler O'Bryen 1853-1928' by James K. Watson

This initiative proved successful but it posed a problem – where could beekeepers find buyers for their honey. The CDB offered to buy everything offered for sale by beekeepers from the remotest parts of rural Ireland and provided special boxes for transporting the honey harvest to Dublin, all under the supervision of 'The Bee Man'.

In the 6th Annual Report of the CDB it stated: "There is every reason to believe that the great majority of those who have adopted improved methods of beekeeping with the assistance of the Board, are satisfied with the results so far obtained and it is anticipated that the number of beekeepers will be largely increased."

It added that 104 hives had been supplied to beekeepers and that, in one case, a farmer had paid his farm rent from honey sales.

The Board promised to buy all available honey but they needed to find buyers for selling on the annual liquid harvest. It was decided to make contact with a successful young shopkeeper in England, Thomas Lipton, the son of Irish parents who left Monaghan for Glasgow during the Famine.

Young Lipton started off with a small grocery store and progressed to growing an international business. He was a millionaire by the age of 30 and in 1880 he decided to make tea available at affordable prices by investing in a tea plantation in Ceylon (later Sri Lanka) and creating the Liptons brand.

Lipton wrote to the Board, to say the Irish honey was selling remarkably well and requesting further supplies.

He was knighted in 1891. He owned a succession of yachts, all named 'Shamrock' and competed in the Admiral's Cup on several occasions but winning eluded him.

Lipton's inspectors were sent to Dublin to inspect the honey on offer. All of it was accepted and so Irish honey was sold in the growing Lipton chain of shops.

The CDB reported: "Mr. Lipton's action in the matter... will be of much service to beekeepers in the West of Ireland, and it is hoped that his cheerfully undertaken experiment will be satisfactory from a financial point of view to justify him in continuing to buy in future years on commercial principles apart from a benevolent motive."

In one year 3,002 sections and 431 pounds of honey were purchased by the CDB from beekeepers for £96 and sold on to by then Sir Thomas Lipton for £109. It resulted in a loss for the Board as expenses for bottles, crates and freight came to a total of £30. But the overall objective had been achieved.

Lipton went on to develop the world's leading Lipton tea brand and sold Irish honey in his shops. When he died in 1931 he left a substantial amount of his money to aid the poor of Glasgow and for the building of hospitals. His business motto was: "Work hard, deal honestly, be enterprising, exercise careful judgement, advertise freely but judiciously."

"He was the supreme benefactor of the beekeepers of Ireland," wrote Watson.

Sir Thomas Johnstone Lipton (1848-1931).
Source: US Library of Congress / Wikimedia Commons

# HONEY & HEALTH

Pure honey consists mainly of sugar but also includes:

- antioxidants
- vitamins
- iron
- zinc

Honey, according to the Mayo Clinic, the American medical centre which employs over 4,500 physicians and scientists, has several attributes and:

- can act as a reliable cough suppressant
- might offer antidepressant and anti-anxiety benefits
- could be associated with reduced risk of heart disease
- assists with healing of wounds, particularly in burns
- might help relieve gastrointestinal conditions

It is advised that honey should not be given to children under the age of 1 year.

# CHAPTER 5

# THE WAGGLE DANCE

Two bees at the entrance to David Geoghegan's 'bee bed' in Co. Galway.

One of the most fascinating discoveries about how bees find pollen and nectar in the vicinity of their hives was made by Karl Von Frisch, an Austrian academic.

Born in 1886 in Vienna he studied medicine, philosophy and zoology. He obtained a university teaching certificate in Zoology and comparative anatomy at the Zoological Institute at the University of Munich. He returned to teach there in the 1950s.

Early in his career Von Frisch established that after bees find nectar in a flower they return to the hive and perform a dance for the prime purpose of communicating to other bees in the hive the exact location of the nectar.

The dance takes place before the bee offloads her 'honey sack' in the hive. On learning the location, bees leave the hive with the knowledge that they have the right directions.

It is believed that the bee doing the dance also gives off a smell of the nectar she collected, and this also assists the bees watching the dance to further identify the location.

This has become known as the 'waggle dance.' It has the broad outline of the graph in page 46.

Austrian ethologist Karl von Frisch (1886 – 1982).

> *"The tail-wagging dance not only indicates distance but also gives the direction," – Von Frisch*

In his book *Decoding the Language of the Bee*, Von Frisch also explains that scent is a simple but effective method of communication, however it only attains its full significance in combination with other triggers.

Von Frisch explained that bees also engage in two dances. The 'round' dance is a signal that invites occupants of the hive to search the immediate vicinity of the hive. "The tail-wagging dance sends them to greater distances, not infrequently several kilometres."

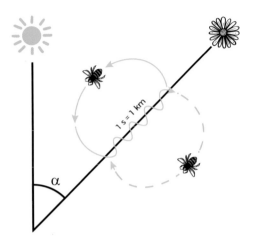

The 'waggle dance' graph.

The key features of the dance include:

- Distance is 'messaged' by the number of oscillations in the centre of the diagram.

- Direction is measured by the angle at which the waggle is performed relative to sun.

- When the other bees leave the hive they know from both the angle of the sun and the 'waggling' where the food source is.

"Those hours at the observation hive when the bees revealed this secret to me remain unforgettable," Von Frisch admitted.

"The fascinating thing is that the angle between the position of the sun and the dancer's path to the goal is expressed by the dancer in the darkness of the hive, on the vertical surface of the comb, as an angular deflection from the vertical."

What is truly amazing is that the bee is able to transpose the angle to a different area of sense perception.

A significant conundrum for Von Frisch in his research was sense perception and questions about time and space.

*"When bees use the sun as a compass during their own flights as well as to inform their comrades, one difficulty arises: With the advancing hour of the day, the sun's position changes, and one would imagine that it can serve as a geographic marker for a short time only."*

The scientist became concerned that he was faced with an aspect of his research for which the answer would elude him: "I had long contemplated an experiment whose execution was postponed from one year to the next by the feeling that it would not amount to much."

But Von Frisch persisted.

Early one morning in the autumn of 1949 he sealed the entrance to his observation hive at Brunnwinkl on the shores of Lake Wolfgang in Austria. He then took it across the lake and placed it in a location some 5 kilometers away, unknown terrain for the bees. Von Frisch had numbered 29 of the bees who had visited a feeding place the previous day from their original location and 200m to the west of their new location.

He placed four feeding bowls with the scent of the former feeding location and placed them exactly 200m from the hive, one to the west and the others to the east, north and south. He then unsealed the entrance to the hive.

Of the 29 marked bees, 27 found the bowls within 3 hours, 5 in the south, 1 in the north, 1 in the east and 20 in the west.

On arrival back at the hive the 29 bees were caught and prevented from waggle dancing to assist the other bees.

The previous day the sun was to the west but in the new location it was to the southeast of the hive.

"Only the sun could have guided those who arrived," he proclaimed.

Von Frisch repeated the trial many times in many modifications and became fully satisfied that bees familiarise themselves with the daily movements of the sun to their hives and by calculating the hour of day, use the sun as a compass.

Karl von Frisch was one of three to be awarded The Nobel Prize in Physiology or Medicine in 1973. Along with Nikolas Tinbergen and Konrad Lorenz, he received the award for 'pioneering contributions in ethnology by studying animal behaviour'. He died in 1982.

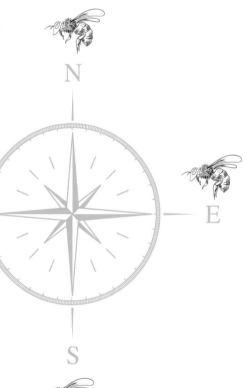

# CHAPTER 6

# IS IT REAL HONEY IN THE JAR?

What the honeybee produces isn't always what you get in a jar of honey.

In 2011 Andrew Schneider, a Pulitzer-winning journalist, claimed that "more than three-fourths of the honey sold in US grocery stores isn't exactly what the bees produce". He had conducted an investigation for *Food Safety News* based on 62 jars and other receptacles across several American states and submitted them for analysis to Vaughn Bryant, a leading expert on pollen and a professor at Texas A & M University.

Bryant, also invited to analyse pollen from bees at The White House by Michelle Obama, revealed:

- 100 per cent of the honey sampled from three leading drug stores had no pollen

- Honey packed in small individual portions at fast food outlets had the pollen removed

- 77 per cent of honey sampled from major food stores had the pollen filtered out

- 100 per cent of samples purchased at farmers markets and co-ops had the expected amount of pollen.

The Food & Drug Administration (FDA) was quoted as saying that it did not consider 'ultra-filtered honey' to be honey.

"It's no secret to anyone in the business that the only reason all the pollen is filtered out is to hide where it initially came from and the fact is that in almost all cases, that is China," Richard Adee, a leading beekeeper with 80,000 hives producing 7 million pounds of honey, told Schneider for *Food Safety News* when the investigation was complete.

## KEY FACTS ABOUT BEES

Bees will fly up to 5 miles from their hive to collect nectar from flowers.

In just one journey a bee will collect nectar from up to 100 flowers.

◀ *Opposite:* Peter Morrissey's hand holding a jar of his own brand of honey in Claddaghduff, north Connemara.

## KEY FACTS
## ABOUT BEES

Bees know when bad weather is on the way and they retreat into the hive.

The publication asked Kathy Edan, a dietician at the College of The Cross in Worcester, Massachusetts if consumers should care if the honey they purchase had its pollen content removed: "Raw honey is thought to have many medicinal properties. Stomach ailments, anaemia and allergies are just a few conditions that may be improved by consumption of unprocessed honey."

In 2015 The European Commission launched a study to detect honey adulteration across all member states and also Norway and Switzerland. Some 70 samples were collected in Ireland. The objective was to establish the prevalence of honey mislabelled with regard to its geographical and botanical origin, and products presented and declared as honey even though they contained exogenous sugars or sugar products.

Europe is the world's largest importer of honey as its annual production of about 250,00 tonnes of honey annually meets with about 60% of annual demand. China is the world's largest producer.

Some 2,264 samples were collected. Results showed that there was a 14.2 per cent prevalence of suspicion of non-compliant ('what it says on the jar'), honeys as high as 20 per cent in one instance. Findings relating to the different stages of the supply chain showed that the highest level of non-compliance was at the wholesaler stage (17.9 per cent), followed by the retailer (16.3 per cent), packager (13.8 per cent).

The report concluded that there is a need for the harmonising of analytical methods and an acceptance that "no universal method exists that is able to determine all the different types of honey adulterants with sufficient sensitivity and robustness."

Fraud in the food chain was the subject of discussion in the European Parliament in 2013.

According to John Spink and Douglas Moyer (*Understanding Food Fraud*, Michigan State University, 2011) food fraud is a collective term used to encompass the deliberate and intentional substitution, addition, tampering, or misrepresentation of food ingredients, food packaging; or false and misleading statements made about a product for economic gain.

Unlike the USA, the EU has no generally acknowledged definition of food fraud, the current EU legislative framework being largely focused on food safety.

The foods most at risk of fraud were listed as:

- Olive oil

- Fish

- Organic foods

- Milk

- Grains

- Honey and maple syrup

Food fraud is more prevalent when the risk of getting caught is small and the economic gain is big.

**KEY FACTS ABOUT HONEY**

Honey is the only food that has all the nutrients necessary to sustain life.

# CHAPTER 7

# THE HONEY LAUNDERING

I n May 2008, Stefanie Giesselbach was arrested by US federal agents at Chicago's O'Hare International Airport just as she was about to fly home to Germany.

Almost simultaneously, Magnus Von Buddenbrock, who was driving back into Chicago having dropped Giesselbach off for her flight, was waved over and also arrested.

The two Germans were both senior executives of the Alfred L. Wolff Group of Hamburg, one of the world's leading distributors of food ingredients. In 2006, Giesselbach was appointed national sales manager for bee products and posted to the company's Chicago office. Von Buddenbrock was also posted to Chicago from Germany the following year.

It was estimated that some $30 million of honey was imported into the US by the German company in the three years up to 2008.

The pair was arrested on federal charges for allegedly conspiring to import honey illegally from China. An informant within the company told US Immigration & Customs Enforcement agents that "it was common knowledge among company executives...that shipments of imported honey frequently contaminated with antibiotics" were banned by the US Food and Drug Administration (FDA).

The US had imposed anti-dumping duties on the import of honey from China in mid-2007. This followed an import alert by the FDA five years previously about honey containing chloramphenicol, an antibiotic not approved for use in producing animals, including bees. Chinese beekeepers, however, were widely using the antibiotic to eradicate diseases and infections in bee hives. The anti-dumping duties which were imposed had a default rate of 221 per cent.

Matt Gauder, a special agent with the US Department of Homeland Security, filed an affidavit in which he declared that the ALW Food group "functioned as a single, integrated criminal organisation that

### KEY FACTS ABOUT HONEY

One ounce of honey is produced from worker bees doing about 1500 round trips.

◄ *Opposite:* Filtering honey from the honeycomb to remove large items of debris such as insect parts and pieces of wax.

conducted its activities in different geographical locales with one unified, overriding purpose – to fraudulently import Chinese-origin honey into the United States to avoid anti-dumping duties."

He went further: I believe it is accurate to like the components of the ALW Food Group to the different components of a vertically integrated narcotics enterprise in which one group grows and harvests coco leaves in Peru, another processes it into cocaine paste in Bolivia, another transports it to Columbia where it is pressed in bricks for export, another tranships it through Mexico to Chicago, where the last component distributes it to the purchasers in retail quantities collecting the proceeds and financing the operation."

The charges were that between 2002 and 2008 ALW Food Group acted as importer for approximately 446 falsely declared entries with a value of just over $30 million including 180 declared as Indian-origin, 163 declared as Russian-origin and other orders as having their origins in Indonesia, Mongolia and the Philippines.

One consignment was returned by a vigilant US buyer in 2006 as it was discovered to be contaminated. But a Wolff representative sold it to a buyer in Texas at a deep discount, who the vendors nicknamed "The Garbage Can" because he knew exactly what he was purchasing.

The whole scam was aimed at avoiding antidumping duties of $59,044,726.

Giesselback and Von Buddenbrock were charged with importing honey – knowing it was mislabelled and adulterated - into the US.

Most of the accused have eluded the US legal system but are on the 'wanted list' of Interpol.

Shortly after the scandal Alfred L Wolff Group no longer existed. It was acquired by a company called Norevo GbMH. Agents from ICE claimed the transaction was a sham and it was simply business as usual with the same player.

Von Buddenbrock was placed under house arrest for six months. Giesselback was jailed for one year and one day. One of the investigators described her as a marionette whose puppet master was Alexander Wolff, CEO, ALW Germany.

In June 2016, there was a massive seizure of counterfeit honey in the Chicago suburbs. Homeland Security Investigations and Customs and Border Protections seized 60 tons of fake honey, which is now stored in a government warehouse on the Texas/Mexico border. It was the largest food fraud investigation in U.S. history.

# CHAPTER 8

# A BAD BUZZ FOR BEES

Bees have always faced threats but during the winter of 2006-2007 beekeepers across the United States noticed something quite alarming happening. Worker bees departed their hives, leaving behind the queen and stores of honey, never to return.

What later became know as 'Colony Collapse Disorder' wiped out between 30 and 90 per cent of hives: "…as many as 50 per cent of all affected colonies demonstrated symptoms inconsistent with any known causes of honey bee death," according the United States Environmental Protection Agency (EPA).

The main characteristics were sudden loss of a colony's worker bee population with very few dead bees found near the colony, the queen and her brood of young bees remained with honey and pollen reserves. However, without worker bees vital reserves cannot be replaced.

A key indicator of bee health is the level of survival of colonies during winter months. The EPA has reported that the number of hives not surviving winters in the US has averaged 28.7 per cent since 2006-2007 and this dropped to 23.1 per cent during the winter of 2015-2016. Losses attributed to CCD stood at 60 per cent in 2008 and fell to just over 31 per cent in 2013.

But just as the problem seemed to be abating the winter of 2017-2018 marked the worst year on record for US beekeepers: "Over the past winter, 37 per cent of honeybee colonies were lost to beekeepers, the worst decline recorded in the 13-year history of a nationwide survey… overall, 40 per cent of colonies died off over the entire year to April, which is above the 38 per cent since the survey began," according to The Guardian newspaper.

Geoffrey Williams, assistant professor of entomology at Auburn University and co-author of the annual honeybee survey carried out by the Bee Informed Partnership, a not-for-profit group led by the University of Maryland, said: "It's disconcerting that we're still seeing

## KEY FACTS ABOUT BEES

Up to 50,000 bees will live in a hive in summer time (and as few as 10,000 in winter).

◄ *Opposite:* Passionate environmentalist, Fr Simon Sleeman, preparing the smoker used to calm and control the colony during an inspection in his apiary at Glenstal Abbey, Co. Limerick.

elevated losses after over a decade of survey and quite intense work to try to understand and reduce colony loss."

Meanwhile in Europe, a study in the winter of 2017-18 found the number of honey bee colonies fell by 16 per cent across 38 countries. The study carried out by the University of Strathclyde surveyed 25,363 beekeepers across 36 countries. From a total of 544,879 colonies at the start of winter just under 90,000 were lost. The rate of losses was down from 20.9 per cent in 2016-17 but higher than the loss of 12 per cent in 2015-16.

Losses were above average in counties Mayo, Galway and Cork and also in Northern Ireland.

An overview of the possible causes of the Colony Collapse Disorder phenomenon.

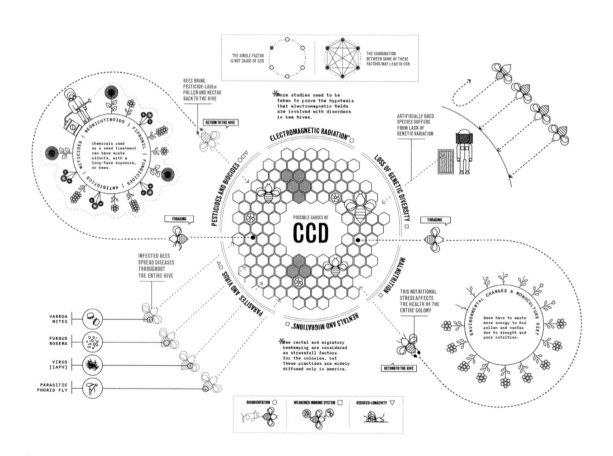

# WHAT'S ALL THE BUZZ ABOUT?

## Total US managed honey bee colonies loss estimates

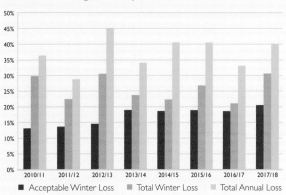

- ■ Acceptable Winter Loss
- ■ Total Winter Loss
- ■ Total Annual Loss

## Honey bee winter losses in Europe

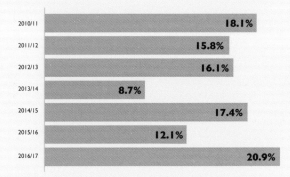

| | |
|---|---|
| 2010/11 | 18.1% |
| 2011/12 | 15.8% |
| 2012/13 | 16.1% |
| 2013/14 | 8.7% |
| 2014/15 | 17.4% |
| 2015/16 | 12.1% |
| 2016/17 | 20.9% |

## 37%

of the US hives did not survive winter during the 2017/18 season

## 16%

is the number of honey bee colonies that fell across 38 European countries during the 2017/18 season.

That means a total of

## 90,000 lost colonies

## Ireland

Losses were above average in counties Mayo, Galway and Cork and also in Northern Ireland.

# VARROA MITES

The varroa mite (*Varroa destructoris*) is an invasive species from Asia which has destroyed bee colonies all over the world. About the size of a pin head, this mite feeds on the circulatory fluid of bees and brood (bee larvae). Nearly all hive inspections by beekeepers include checking for the existence of varroa, aided sometimes by using a magnifying glass. A number of treatments are available but early detection is key.

Varroa mites threaten agricultural pollination directly by weakening and destroying bee colonies.

A varroa mite on the back of a bee (centre) in a hive.

# CHAPTER 9

# SLEEPING WITH BEES

# DAVID GEOGHEGAN

'I lie on the hive and felt microvibration. It was a feeling that buzzing wires and something slightly pushes in the back. Then I got dizzy from the smell of lime, buckwheat, propolis and I fell asleep. I slept for ten minutes, but it felt like after a full night's rest! '

When David Geoghegan read this account by Russian keeper Vladimir Megre, he couldn't resist trying it out. The trained carpenter, organic farmer and honey producer fitted out his garden retreat overlooking Lough Corrib in Co. Galway, with his very own "bee bed" – akin to a little bit of heaven on earth.

Every day, for five or ten minutes, Geoghegan retreats behind the full length maroon curtains to lie on the mattress laid above three of his hives in his large wooden shed. The hives are fitted with exits to the shed's exterior, similar to "cat flaps".

Even in winter, the slight heat is "better than any electric blanket", he says. The honeyed hum and vibration from thousands of wings sends him into a slumber which is "just as good as eight hours at night", he says.

The soothing sound effect is similar to camping at night beside the sea, and, as Megre had noted, problems disappear...

Geoghegan has been a native Irish honeybee keeper for decades, just as his father was before him. He has up to 80 productive hives on his organic vegetable farm out the Glann road beyond Oughterard, where he can name the lake's islands, such as Inis Sean Bó and Rua Oileán, to compass points west, east and south.

### KEY FACTS ABOUT BEES

The buzz of a bee is made by its wings flapping 200 times per second.

◄ *Opposite:* Keeper David Geoghegan in his 'bee bed' designed and built at his home overlooking Lough Corrib in Co. Galway.

'Anything to do with keeping bees cannot be done at speed,' Geoghegan explains, as he escorts me into his sterilised honey room, where dozens of buckets, each 30lbs (13.6 kilos) weight are stacked neatly on shelves.

His Connemara honey is processed with intense care, starting with a settlement tank where the honey sinks and wax, pollen and propolis – the latter known as "bee glue" and comprising resin, wax and essential oils – will rise to the top.

At its final stage, he fills the jars, and labels them, completing up to 100 in an hour as he listens to music.

Foraging for his hives is particularly rich around Lough Corrib, where bluebell, wood violet and primrose grow in woodlands, wild angelica and purple loosestrife flourish along the rocky shore, and fenlands support marsh orchid and meadowthistle.

However, Geoghegan's bees also enjoy meadowsweet, blackberry briars, holly, sycamore, lime trees, heather, fuschia, dandelions and cotoneaster.

He produces a separate honey from ivy, which has healing properties and is rich in iodine. One owner of a horse with an injured leg contacted him, and he sent a pot. He shows me photographs of how the large gash healed up completely in three months.

His bee bed is his retreat after a full day on the hives and it is in his garden, where he grows everything from potatoes and carrots to onions and beetroot.

'It's not just sound and the sense of vibration, but there's also a smell which is slightly musty, different to honey, and must be made up of pollen, and propolis and all the good stuff,' he says.

'About 80 per cent of what they bring in is moisture, and has to be

KEY FACTS
ABOUT BEES

Bees operate the highest standards of cleanliness inside the hive.

David Geoghegan outside his home pointing at the entrance of the 'bee bed'.

## KEY FACTS ABOUT BEES

The hive is made up of one queen, worker bees and drones.

fanned out to get the moisture level correct in the honey, so you can imagine the heat generated by all that shaking and shimmering,' he says.

'Even in winter, they might just go out for water or on a cleansing flight or picking up bits of pollen and nectar from late flowers, they would be moving around to maintain heat in the cluster - a bit like how you see the penguins huddled together in Antarctica,' he says.

Geoghegan even has a mirror fitted outside the window, aimed at the bee doors to see how they are doing. On his wall is a sign that reads 'life is like riding a bicycle – to keep your balance, you must keep moving'.

'I just love bees, and their whole philosophy, and I would do anything for the native Irish honeybee which seems to be resisting the Varroa mite without any treatment,' he says. 'Bees are so focused, they have no greed, no ego. If we were as concerned about our planet as they are about their colony, we'd all be in a better place...'

'Bees are so focused, they have no greed, no ego. If we were as concerned about our planet as they are about their colony, we'd all be in a better place...'

# CHAPTER 10

# SCIENCE HELPING THE WILD BEES

# GRACE MCCORMACK

reland's native wild honeybee should be granting Prof Grace McCormack a free pass from stings – for life. The NUI Galway scientist has done much to spread awareness about its value, not least the fact that it still exists.

Wild colonies of honeybee have been all but wiped out in most of the rest of northern Europe, but Ireland's sub-species, *Apis mellifera mellifera*, is surviving in its pure form.

Research led by Prof McCormack and colleagues at NUIG and Limerick Institute of Technology, which was published in 2017, confirmed that it is not extinct in Ireland.

Bizarrely, honeybees are not a protected species, due to EU trade laws and Ireland's own legislation which classifies them as domestic animals. Yet there is every reason for them to be given protected status, given the threats posed by pesticides, imports of other strains of honeybees, and the consequent spread of the Varroa parasite, which can destroy entire colonies in several years.

Even Ireland's all-island pollinator plan doesn't cut honeybees much slack. It has not recognised the honeybee as a wild pollinator, Prof McCormack points out. State agencies aren't as interested as they should be in its future, and yet it could prove to be a very important livestock for farmers who don't necessarily want to produce beef.

When the Native Irish Honeybee Society (NIHBS) was formed in 2012, it turned to Prof McCormack in NUIG's school of natural

## KEY FACTS ABOUT HONEY

A hive of honeybees can produce up to 70 jars of honey but this depends on the health of the hive and weather conditions.

◀ *Opposite:* Prof Grace McCormack of NUI Galway with the hives kept at an apiary in Terryland, overlooking the river Corrib in Galway city.

### KEY FACTS ABOUT BEES

Worker bees are all female. They are the honey bees we see flying around collecting pollen and nectar from flowers.

sciences for help in providing scientific evidence in support of *A. m. mellifera* conservation and improvement.

One of their first joint ventures was to establish a breeding programme which could increase the number of honeybees in Ireland resistant to the Varroa mite. In addition McCormack decided to follow up on reports of honeybees living in the wild from beekeepers and members of the public. Working with PhD student Keith Browne, Prof McCormack issued an appeal to citizen scientists in 2015 to report wild honeybee colonies.

The appeal was a great success, as over 200 reports of honeybee colonies in buildings, trees, walls and other cavities, extending from Dublin to Galway to Kerry to Fermanagh, were submitted.

Even better, it appeared that some of the wild free-living colonies had survived for over three years without human intervention – suggesting they had a resistance to Varroa, which can wipe out a colony within one to two years unless chemically treated.

A new online citizen survey was initiated in May, 2019, in collaboration with NIHBS and with the Federation of Irish Beekeeping Associations, and in collaboration with the National Biodiversity Data Centre. It is the first of its type in Europe, and has been yielding good results.

Prof McCormack keeps bees herself - the university has established an apiary at Terryland, overlooking the river Corrib, started with

nine hives donated by native Irish beekeepers. She also maintains several hives at her home in Ballinderreen, south Galway, along with neighbouring farmer PJ Martyn at Mulrook.

As PJ says, trees, gaps in walls, particular shrubs, roofs of old buildings, inside sheds all provide a haven. He is so passionate about bees that he knows what weather they like, why they don't like bananas, how their scouts find new places to swarm, and also why they don't like having their photograph taken. "They don't bother you if you don't bother them," he says.

Farmers are vital for the future of the wild Irish honeybee, Prof McCormack says. Adequate forage is vital, and Ireland has never been the ideal environment, she notes. Some of the earliest reports of honeybees, which came from Britain, noted that vegetation was sparse.

However, increased interest in beekeeping is being matched by increased awareness. Cultivating "bee-friendly" plants and leaving some hedgerows and grass edges free to grow and flower enriches the environment for honeybees and other pollinators.

Prof McCormack's aim is now to sequence the genome of the wild Irish honeybee, which may give indications in relation to its resistance to Varroa and may help to trace its ancestry. Much depends on finance – ironically, the public enthusiasm and goodwill for such work on the tiny animal is not always matched by suitable funding streams...

# CHAPTER 11

# BEES CAN BE GRUMPY TOO

# GERARD COYNE

I f Gerard Coyne enjoyed a past life, it may have been spent as a honeybee or a zoologist, or both...

Had Austrian scientist and Nobel prize winner Karl Ritter von Frisch not discovered the 'waggle dance', it would certainly have been observed first by Coyne.

There is little about the complex behaviour of bees that Coyne does not know, and he cannot remember a time when he wasn't besotted.

'There were bees everywhere when I was growing up, and most farms had a couple of hives,' Coyne, a farmer from Ballynew, Moyard in north Connemara, recalls.

He paints one particular postcard image from the past.

'One day my father and uncle were at the hay and we were all going in for the cup of tea – I was about nine or ten.'

'My father wondered if there was anything sweet in the house and there wasn't. So my uncle lit his pipe, opened a hive and took out some honey... no gear on him, just the smoke from his tobacco...'

'I never could forget that taste of fresh honey on mother's home-made bread...'

'Back in those days, they would have time to observe the bees, and nearly knew when they were going to swarm, but they wouldn't disturb the hives till the end of each year,' he says. 'It was probably healthier for the bees. We'd be hanging around to get a finger into tasting the honey coming out! And I found if I was passing a hive, I always wanted to take a look...'

## KEY FACTS ABOUT BEES

Worker bees live for between 4 and 6 weeks and they account for about 98 per cent of the bees in a hive.

◄ *Opposite:* Gerard Coyne with the hives he keeps at an apiary in Moyard, north Connemara.

And Coyne still does that, whether it is among his hives at home, or at Ballynahinch Castle Hotel, or in any of the apiaries maintained by his many students. He is a founder member of the Native Irish Honey Bee Society, dedicated to support the much undervalued *Apis mellifera mellifera*.

He is also passionate about dogs, and compares the bee to the Border Collie in its behavioural response.

'It is all about taking your time, and so if you are in a hurry, or you are rough, you can forget it,' he laughs, his large hands pointing to spots on his head and arms where he has been stung.

'I always wear the suit, but I even keep my hair long in the summer, just in case...'

'Weather is also a factor, because bees can have their grumpy times,' he says. 'Bees don't have the same temperament every day'.

Planning and notekeeping are essential, he says, and he keeps regular diaries.

'You have to know what you are going to do before you approach a hive,' he advises.

Coyne also keeps meticulous records of the native Irish honeybee queens which he breeds, and has nicknames for them, related to townlands where they might have been found.

'So I have 'P' for Protestant, because this queen was originally found in the grounds of the Church of Ireland in Moyard, and then I have a group

KEY FACTS
ABOUT BEES

The tiny bee brain has a capability to learn, remember and calculate distance.

91

called 'na Piarsaigh', found by a keeper named Paddy Finnerty near Padraig Pearse's cottage in Rosmuc,' Coyne says.

Another group of queens are named 'Agnes' after the owner of a cottage where he located a specimen.

The resilience of the native Irish honeybee, and how it has adapted since the Ice Age, is still a marvel to him, and he sent DNA records to Prof Grace McCormack of NUI Galway for her research.

As for their work ethic, it is phenomenal, he says – 'the foraging can be tough as the season is short, so they work from 6am to 11pm in the summer, and each townland has a different type of crop.'

Clover provides some of the best forage, and so chemical nitrogen treatments to produce 'pristine' pasture are of no benefit to the bee. He also believes there should be penalties imposed for illegal imports of bees.

'We had a ban in the 1990s when the Varroa mite arrived, but then it was lifted,' he says. 'I just can't understand how little appreciation the State seems to have of the native Irish honeybee...'

Coyne says that it took him 30 years to understand the art of artificial swarming and the fact that 'we were tricking the bees into thinking they had swarmed', which he once regarded as 'something of a miracle – like the loaves and fishes'.

'It doesn't always work, but it really is the only time you can actually trick bees', he says.

For Coyne, happiness is listening to the hum, watching the activity around hives of an afternoon when time stands still.

# SWARMING

*Apis mellifera mellifera* queen.

Honeycomb of honey bees with eggs and larvae.
The walls of the cells have been removed. The larvae
(drones) are about 3 or 4 days old.

*"A swarm of May is worth a load of hay
A swarm in June is worth a silver spoon
A swarm in July isn't worth a fly"*

This is an old saying that has been handed down by generations of beekeepers to explain that a new colony as a result of swarming will produce honey the earlier in the year it happens.

When a hive becomes overpopulated food supplies have to be shared by more bees and this can threaten the entire population. This situation prompts the hive's worker bees to take action.

The swarming procedure starts when the workers identify selected eggs that the queen has laid and feed them with royal jelly. This accelerates the birth of a new queen.

The next stage is when a large number of the bees depart the hive in unison. They prompt the old queen to join them and quite quickly the departed queen will land in a nearby location and she will be surrounded by her bees. Meanwhile a small number of her 'scouts' (worker bees) fly off in search of a new 'home.'

Sometimes the temporary location can be rather inconvenient for people going about their daily business...

In July 2019 a swarm of bees descended on a flower box in Limerick city, causing, in the words of one report, 'panic.' Two local beekeepers arrived on the scene and took charge, removing the swarm.

Bee swarm on a bicycle.

Beekeepers in Ireland are on alert from April onwards and regular checking of the hives for inspect the existence and development of queen larvae is the best way to find out if swarming is immiment.

When a hive swarms the new location is usually not far away and beekeepers on good terms with their neighbours are likely to be alerted about 'a lot of bees on one of my apple trees' or wherever. Inconvenient locations for swarming bees include chimneys, attics, high up on tall trees, garden sheds and disbanded vehicles.

Beekeepers will usually have an empty hive ready to provide a new home for the swarm.

And while all this is happening the bees that remained in the hive now tend to their new young queen. In time, this queen starts laying, the worker bees continue their flights for nectar and pollen. And if the integration of the new queen is successful the colony will grow back up to some 50,000 bees in mid-summer and food reserves will be stored up for the winter.

# CHAPTER 12

# WHO'S KEEPING WHO?

# FR SIMON SLEEMAN

I have looked after the monastery bees for the last forty years - or rather I should say, they have 'looked after me', keeping me company through the many ups and downs of life. I use the phrase, 'looked after' advisedly - at an earlier stage I used the word 'manage' and described myself as a 'beekeeper' both of which I now see as misnomers.

Bees are not domesticated nor are they dependent on us for their welfare as cattle or sheep are - they are wild insects whose natural habitat is a hole in a tree - nor do we keep them - most 'beekeepers' do their best to 'manage' them. Over the years we have complicated the art of looking after bees and now it can be a challenge to just keep a hive of bees alive.

I first developed an interest in bees when I was studying in Dublin and staying in a hostel in Palmerston Park. My room overlooked the well-kept kitchen garden with its two beehives. Periodically, Jack O'Brien, a retired guard, came to inspect the hives. He wore a suit and tie and no protective gear. I peered out from the safety of my room. There was something about the way he worked with the bees that put them at ease. He got the odd sting, but it never bothered him. He was my first teacher.

When I returned to Glenstal, I was determined to start my own apiary. The abbot agreed to the purchase of six hives. Br Eugene the bursar at the time, knew of an American woman living in Killaloe who was moving back to the USA and selling her equipment. We went

### KEY FACTS ABOUT BEES

The worker bees are the only members of the hive with a stinger.

◄ *Opposite:* Fr Simon Sleeman, at Glenstal Abbey, working in his apiary.

to investigate. She and her husband were fastidious eaters. They never confused their bodies by eating protein and carbohydrate at the same meal - no fish and chips. They ate bread and honey for breakfast, but no fry. They ate so much honey that they imported it by the barrel. They served us tea, honey and brown bread and we did the deal, and as we began to load the six cedar hives she said, 'take the lot', that included many more hives, an extractor, feeders, bee suit - everything needed to set up an apiary! I was set up for a life of beekeeping.

Subsequently I have thought a lot about that barrel of honey - I sell some honey in the Glenstal shop, but due to the vicissitudes of the weather I can never produce enough to supply the monks, not to mind the shop. I heard it suggested that if you add a little holy water to a barrel of water it all becomes holy. I wondered could the same principle apply - if I imported a barrel of New Zealand honey and added a jar of Glenstal honey... could I sell it all as Glenstal honey? Even my conscience wouldn't cope with that sleight of hand.

Having completed my beginners course in Gormanston College, I began my beekeeping career, full of enthusiasm about how I would manage my bees. And I was definitely 'keeping them' at that time. I was an 'interventionist beekeeper, aggressively managing my bees - inspecting them and manipulating with little regard for the devastation as I ripped apart their home every ten days during the summer months. I wanted them to produce as much honey as possible - totally ignoring the fact that their plan was quite different - they simply want to survive and reproduce.

Some years later I went to Ampleforth Abbey to study theology and took the opportunity to visit the most famous beekeeper in the world, Br Adam in Buckfast. He was already in his eighties, but still spent a full day (5.30 am start) with his bees. He had little time for talking about his theories but let me work with his wonderful assistant Peter Grace. Peter knew Br Adam's systems and taught me all he knew.

It was not long after this, that my bees contracted American Foul Brood - a notifiable disease. The Department of Agriculture informed me that my hives would have to be destroyed - officials arrived and poured petrol into the hives and the fumes killed the bees. The hives were saved, but had to be scorched.

KEY FACTS
ABOUT BEES

It takes about three
weeks for eggs laid by
the queen to develop
into adults bees.

I was reluctant to start again. Later that summer I was giving a grind in biology when there was a knock at the door. Someone was looking for me... something to do with bees. His name was Joe. I peered under the arch and there was a battered, white hiace van and beside it a dishevelled individual with a week's stubble but with a very warm and open face. I introduced myself. He told me he was a beekeeper over in Bridgetown. He had heard about my bees. Then he uttered the unforgettable words, 'no beekeeper should be without bees... I have two hives in the back of the van for you'. I could not believe it - he had somehow heard my bees were dead and brought me two of his precious colonies! I had no choice but to start up again. I later discovered Joe was a bachelor and has since died. I pray for him.

I am an undisciplined beekeeper. One of the first lessons I was taught is that all your equipment should be interchangeable. Instead of obeying this reasonable injunction I have five types of hive all of which require different equipment. I have the classic National Hive, the Commercial Hive, the Rose Hive (all boxes are the same), the Langstroth Hive and a Top Bar Hive. Some of my hives are made of wood others of styrofoam.

I am now older and more respectful of the bees and their extraordinary adaptations to life on this earth. It has taken me nearly 40 years to repent (which means to pay attention) and change my ways. I don't know what prompted this change - maybe it was the fact that modern management techniques have contributed to the decline of bees and earned 'beekeeping' the dubious honour of being one of the first industrial agriculture systems to almost collapse. We blame mites, the weather, farmers and some of this is accurate but not all of it. We need to ask ourselves, what is our part in this? The fact is, that many of us have lost the ability to look after, to care for, living things.

For too long I treated my hives as units of production much like dairy farmers talk about cows. Long gone are the days when each cow had a name. We place bees in mono-crops to pollinate plant species and expect them to thrive on a diet of one food type. Drones (male bees) are often regarded as lazy, good for nothings except to mate with the

queen, neglecting the vital role they play in the colony. We only provide worker bee wax foundation reducing the number of drones. We tend to work against them rather than with them, focusing on making life easier and more profitable for the beekeeper rather than the bee.

But there was a more important moment for me five years ago. It was a summer's day and a worker bee was resting at the hive entrance and I looked at it, looked at it again, and saw a bee, saw a bee for the first time. I stood there, transfixed and marvelled at this extraordinary creature that I had missed for forty years - its beauty and design, fashioned over 50 million years. That is 48 million years longer than we have been on the planet. How had I not seen it before? I was blind for all those years, thinking I was a 'beekeeper'.

**Fr Simon Sleeman**

# CHAPTER 13

# THE BEE SANCTUARY OF LIMERICK

# ST MARY'S PARISH MEN'S SHED

Black honeybees feast under a very special piece of street art in Limerick city. A triptych of the late Cranberries singer Dolores O'Riordan overlooks a wildflower meadow provided for pollinators by the local authority.

Ger Ryan, Pat Collins and fellow members of St Mary's Parish Men's Shed are almost as proud of the new artwork sprayed on a gable end of St Nicholas's Street by Dublin street artist Aches, as they are of their apiary.

A graffiti image of Limerick actress Constance Smith, who was cast in over 30 films in Hollywood in the 1950s, bookends the streetscape in Limerick's medieval quarter. Colonies of the native Irish honeybee have "reserved dining" from the wildflower crop close by, but they know they can also take off down the river Shannon for dessert.

'We got our first queen from a keeper in Clonlara, and we built the hives ourselves,' Ryan and Collins explain, walking down the garden of the men's shed premises.

'We got our first swarm in a copper beech tree across the road, and we learned how to merge two colonies,' they explain. ' We think that first swarm came from a hive on the roof of Brown Thomas in the city...'

There's been a tradition of keeping in St Mary's -better known as "the parish" – with several hives on the roof of St Munchin's Church of Ireland church for a time, while the Hunt Museum has both a hive and a small "bee loud glade" planted close by.

## KEY FACTS ABOUT BEES

Drones are male bees and their purpose is to mate with the queen.

They have bigger eyes than worker bees, helping them to find the queen.

A drone dies after he mates with the queen.

◀ *Opposite:* Beekeepers Pat Collins, left, and Ger Ryan, right, wearing the protective gear to attend their beehives at St Mary's Parish Men's Shed, Limerick City.

### KEY FACTS ABOUT HONEY

A bee will produce about one tenth of a teaspoon of honey during the 5-6 weeks of her life.

When the St Mary's men's shed opened in 2012, the initial focus was on planting a herb, vegetable and flower garden, with flowers donated by local garden centres. A carpentry bench is fitted with tools for carving Welsh marriage spoons and constructing hulls for local boats such as the Shannon cot and the gandelow.

Ryan is from a family of fishermen, and knows how to pole an angling cot up the weir and how to track eels - and the social impact of restrictions on estuary fishing for salmon over the past decade.

Like Collins and a number of friends in the men's shed group, he has a busy schedule of bodhrán sessions and art classes and other activities, but is fascinated by the life cycle of the native Irish honeybee.

'So we got called out when people saw this ball of bees on a flower stand between Catherine Street and Shannon Street, and a Polish lady who owns a cafe nearby was able to tell us it had a queen as her father had kept bees back in Poland,' Collins says.

The men then installed several hives in an enclosed yard next to the Forty Shilling Almshouses, built in the 17th Century near St John's Castle. A steel door protects this apiary, complete with sliding peep holes to allow people to have a glimpse of the "Bee Sanctuary", as it is called.

'We got 16 jars of honey this year, and didn't go looking for more as we feel the bees need to have something to sustain them,' Collins and Ryan say.

'And what sustains us is watching them come and go, and introducing people to them for the first time. We have suits for people to wear, and it is wonderful to watch the reaction...'

# CHAPTER 14

# STARTING WITH A WILDFLOWER MEADOW

# LESLEY EMIN

If it was a piece of gold from the National Museum of Ireland, Lesley Emin couldn't handle the timber frame more carefully. In a sense it is just as delicate, as she traces her finger over the artistry involved in creating "nectar of Connemara".

"Pure raw Irish honey – that's all" is how her jar label reads, and the contents glisten like captured rays of summer. Emin, science graduate and long-term management consultant from Co. Antrim, opted to pursue a new career as a mountain guide.

She trained with Donegal climber Bren Whelan, and now guides walkers of all grades over and around the Twelve Bens and Maamturks, the bens, the boreens and the beaches of Connemara. The Company of Walkers, as she calls it, also offers expeditions to remote and interesting high places across continental Europe.

Not long after she had moved to live under Cashel Hill, she fell under the spell of keeper Gerard Coyne. She signed up for one of his beginner beekeeping courses, run under the auspices of the Native Irish Honey Bee Society, in Letterfrack, north Connemara.

'I found I had a wildflower meadow here, and that was what sparked my interest,' Emin explains, showing me her apiary. She began with two hives, and now has a third after one of her colonies swarmed.

As anyone who has walked mountains with Emin knows, she has an intimate knowledge of what's underfoot – be it tormentil

## KEY FACTS ABOUT BEES

If a hive is moved even three feet from its original location the bees will find it difficult to find 'home'. But if a hive is moved more than a few miles the bees will re-locate successfully!

◄ *Opposite:* Lesley Emin behind one her beehives in Cashel, Co. Galway.

115

or common butterwort or bog asphodel, and she also has a keen understanding of the composition of rocks beneath.

Therefore, she recognises just how important it is that a colony of at least 10,000 bees per hive should have enough foraging material. She also recognises how dependent her colonies are on surrounding land free from pesticides.

'As if they were actually 'my' bees,' she laughs. 'That's what is so wonderful about it.'

She drops her voice as she approaches her two hives carefully, explaining how bees will sense if there any obstacles, or animate objects, on their flight path. Her first hives were traditional wooden structures, treated with linseed, and she then moved to a polystyrene hive for her third colony.

'Gerard Coyne helped me to set up with two small colonies of queens and bees bred by himself, and he has been very encouraging, and always happy to take a call,' she says.

Emin has two fox terriers, one of which has been stung and isn't so thrilled when he sees her donning her keepers' protective suit.

Sensing that the position of her apiary may not have been ideal for either bee or hound, she cleared an area within a copse of willows and hazel for a more secluded spot.

During 2019, she had a swarm, which resembled what she describes as 'the classic bunch of grapes', suspended from a shrub in her garden. Fortunately she had her beesuit and a third hive to hand.

She took the lid off and moved it close by, got out a stepladder and gently encouraged the the swarm off the branch and into the hive by firmly knocking the shrub with a stick.

'The whole thing just flowed in like treacle... it was quite extraordinary to watch...' she says.

She cites the simple rule for moving a beehive - either fewer than three feet or over three miles.

'The reason for this is quite simple: Bees learn their local area by sight very accurately. If you move the hive over three feet, the flying bees will fly back to the original site, not find the hive and certainly die,' she says.

**KEY FACTS
ABOUT BEES**

Honey bees will fly at about
15 miles an hour

'However, if you move the hive over three miles, the bees will not recognise any of the surrounding area. They will learn their new location. If you move the hive less than three miles, there is a chance that the bees will recognise their old flight area and attempt to return to their old hive position,' she explains.

Emin has produced her first crops of honey – named, appropriately enough, The Company of Bees.

'I still can't get over the fact that this is the natural produce from my wildflower garden...'

# CHAPTER 15

# STUNG ON THE TONGUE

# PETER MORRISSEY

A hint of hawthorn, a touch of clover, a taste of blackberry... keeper Peter Morrissey reckons this is a great combination for wild Irish honey.

'And heather...but usually it is out too late in bloom and the weather had turned,' Morrissey says, his eyes lighting up as he thinks of his hives out at Claddaghduff in north Connemara.

Morrissey, a retired accountant, may have been smitten when he was just a baby. He was in his pram in Kiltimagh, Co. Mayo, when he was stung – on the tongue.

'You can just imagine what it must have been like for my mother, but I had no allergic reaction,' he says.

Beekeeping as a form of domestic economy had been introduced by the Congested Districts Board on the west coast from the early 20th Century, and Kiltimagh was one of the successful clusters.

Turlough Butler O'Bryen – subject of James K Watson's book, *The Bee Man of County Clare* – was welcomed into Kiltimagh by Fr Denis O'Hara, its entrepreneurial priest, Morrissey explains.

'O'Bryen's big task was to persuade people to move over from the old straw skep which had no frames, and harvesting the honey meant killing many bees. He encouraged them to take a more scientific approach, which would produce honey,' he says.

'So an expertise was built up, and I remember my grandmother and an uncle having bees,' he says.

### KEY FACTS ABOUT HONEY

The flavour of honey is determined by the type of flowers the nectar is taken from...clover, heather and blackberry are among the most common in Ireland.

◀ *Opposite:* Beekeeper Peter Morrissey taking care of his hives in Claddaghduff, Co. Galway.

'I pulled two hives out of the granary when I was a teenager and got some honey, and the bug never left me. When I was off boarding in school, my mother and sister had to take the honey out.'

After his retirement, he bought a house in Claddaghduff and fell under the spell of the master, Gerard Coyne.

'Gerard taught me the art of artificial swarming, so you don't lose half your colony. I eventually managed it – after two years of losing bees.'

'My land is very exposed to the Atlantic, so these bees had to be very resilient. I started off with three good colonies in 2017, but two died off over the hard winter and one swarmed.'

'In 2018, I split the one and bought another nucleus from Gerard. And so by 2019, I had three hives and the best year ever, with up to 150 pots of honey.'

'I did have those couple of years when everything went wrong, but I didn't mind as I felt I was learning,' Morrissey says.

What fascinated him in particular was the fact that the bees did not follow textbook behaviour in 2019.

'You have to inspect them every seven days from the beginning of May to the middle of June, because if they are going to swarm the bees will create a queen cell,' he explains.

'On the eighth day, the cell is sealed and they swarm, barring a tempest. That is the theory, but this year they did not swarm on the eighth day.

Morrissey also explains how the eye becomes attuned to the workings of the hive.

'An unmarked new queen has a loping walk... you mark them on the thorax, with a different colour coding for each year... And it is easy to spot a Varroa mite, as it looks like a little crab or a grain of brown sugar.'

The 'game' is what fascinates him about it all, and the ability of bees to adapt.

'It is all about getting the bees to think differently... so you use the smoker, and they fill themselves up with honey and are ready to go, as they think it is a forest fire,' he says.

'Or you mate a virgin queen and she's not laying, or just isn't there at all, and so you put in a test frame with new eggs, day old eggs and larvae, and that gets her broody...

"You come back in ten to twelve days and you find she has been laying like a lunatic, with four or five frames filled with eggs. And of course a queen can lay up to 2,000 eggs a day.'

A hive is a democracy, rather than a dictatorship, Morrissey believes.

'So the queen is like the Taoiseach, as she gives off pheromones [a chemical substance released to influence behaviour] which tell the bees what to do, but she's doomed if she doesn't perform.'

'While the queen is in power, she is all powerful... so it is like politics, because when the workers think they aren't going to survive they plan for her demise and rear a new queen...'

### KEY FACTS ABOUT BEES

The worker bees bring the pollen and nectar back to the hive and it is from here pure honey comes.

'You think about the short life of the worker bee, and it has learned to adapt, while it has taken us so much longer to evolve,' he says.

'So we are hoping that we get a strain of bee that has evolved to resist the Varroa mite... and there are very encouraging signs,' he adds.

'The bees we have here on the west coast of Ireland really are tough out.'

Morrissey says it is 'unbelievably therapeutic', and similar to an endorphin boost from running. During the summer, he loves to observe the bees engaged in their favourite foraging.

'People that have cotoneaster shrubs which are in bloom in May, will get a great idea of bees foraging...'

He also has advice for anyone fed up with stings.

'Some days when the bees are angry and stinging you through the leather gloves, you just leave the frame down for one or two minutes and look at them walking around with the pollen on their back legs... and somehow they seem to become so much calmer.'

'And if you do mishandle them in any way, they certainly let you know!!!'

# BEE STINGS

The HSE: "After stinging someone, bees leave behind their sting and a venomous sac in the wound. This should be removed immediately by scraping it out with something that has a hard edge, such as a bank card... some people can have an immediate and more widespread allergic reaction to being stung. This is known as anaphylactic shock, which sometimes can be fatal. Anaphylactic shock after an insect sting is quite rare, affecting approximately 3 people in 100. It usually only occurs after a wasp sting.

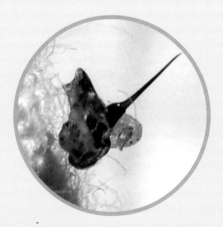

The stinger of a black bee (*Apis mellifera mellifera*) torn from the bee's body and attached to a protective dressing.

# WHAT TO DO AFTER A BEE STING
## 3 SIMPLE STEPS

**1** **REMOVE THE STINGER WITH A DULL-EDGED OBJECT**

Use a blunt object, such a credit card or butter knife, to gently scrape across the affected area. Do not use tweezers, they could squeeze the stinger's venom sack and make symptoms worst.

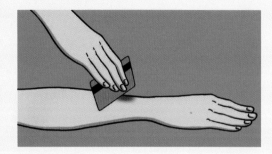

**2** **APPLY A COOL COMPRESS**

Apply a cool compress, such as an ice pack, once the stinger is removed to help aliviate pain. An antihistamine taken orally or applied as a cream can help alleviate itching and swelling.

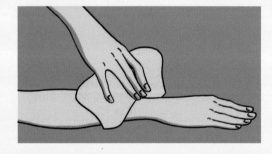

**3** **ELEVATE THE AREA**

Elevate the area, depending on the location of the sting, to help reduce swelling. These symptoms can last between a few hours and a few days.

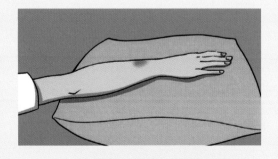

If you are experiencing a more severe reaction such as a feeling of uneasiness, tingling sensations, dizziness, wheezing and difficulty breathing or loss of consciousness...

## GO TO THE ER IMMEDIATELY

# CHAPTER 16

# URBAN BEE SCENE

# DUBLIN CITY HIVES

Honeybees are as sensitive to good property management as any two-legged tenants might be. That's one reason why the work of the 'Schwarmfänger', a network of swarm-catchers in the German capital, Berlin, attracted the recent interest of *The New York Times*.

'We have too many people who keep bees who don't do enough for their bees,' Prof Benedikt Polaczek, lecturer at the Free University of Berlin and head of the city's beekeepers' association, told the newspaper

However, that is not an issue in Dublin, according to keeper Michael Wildes who maintains native Irish honeybee colonies in the capital and beyond.

The Revenue Commissioners and the Department of Agriculture, Food and the Marine are among a number of State agencies in the city with hives, and the Department of Foreign Affairs is planning to join that group.

Michael and Anne Wildes are owners of Tara Hill Honey in Gorey, Co. Wexford. They were approached by Mick Boylan, facilities manager in Agriculture House in Dublin's Kildare Street, after he heard how well hives were doing on rooftops nearby.

'It has been a great success,' Boylan says. 'There are lime trees in Fisheries Yard off Kildare Street, and our honey tastes of that, and we serve it up in our canteen free for anyone who wants it on their porridge or toast.'

### KEY FACTS ABOUT BEES

The queen bee lays up to 2,500 eggs a day. She is the controller of the colony. She is busiest during the summer months. The queen can live up to 6 years.

◀ *Opposite:* An Post's Head of Procurement and Fingal North Dublin Beekeepers Association, Paula Butler, holding a brood frame from the bee colony located on the rooftop of the GPO building in O'Connell Street, Dublin city.

Tara Hill Honey also manages hives at the Web Summit in Milltown, Dublin, and they supply native Irish honeybees to Facebook in Clonee, Co. Meath.

Wildes, a prison officer, manages the hives on the grounds of Shelton Abbey low security prison near Arklow in Co. Wicklow.

'People don't realise there are hives all over Dublin, maintained by An Post on the GPO, at Dublin Airport, and by staff at the Merrion Hotel,' Wildes says.

'Foraging isn't an issue, as bees will fly a three-mile radius for food, and there is an abundance of forage in suburban gardens, and the beautiful trees in the parks,' he says.

The Wildes draw on a lifetime's experience for artificial swarming and other management techniques. Anne Wildes has kept bees since she was ten years old, and came from a long line of keepers in Wexford. The couple use organic treatments for the Varroa mite, believing no colony has sufficient resistance to the parasite.

'It is very rewarding – the hives on the rooftop of Agriculture House in Kildare Street yielded some 70 lbs of honey in 2019,' Michael Wildes says.

The department also has hives at Back Weston campus in Co. Kildare, maintained by agricultural inspector Dr Rachel Wisdom.

▲ Stamps designed by Dublin's Design HQ, based on illustrations by botanical artist Shevaun Doherty, pay tribute to the hardest working insects on the planet and in particular Ireland's native Bumble Bee, Heather Bee and rarer Tawny Mining and Ashy Mining bees. They are produced in an unusual hexagonal format mirroring the cell structure of a bee hive.

# THE TINY MIRACLE WORKERS

"Human beings have fabricated the illusion that in the 21st Century they have the technological prowess to be independent of nature," Achim Steiner, United Nations Environment Programme Executive Director, warned several years ago. "Bees underline the reality that we are more, not less, dependent on nature's services", he added.

And yet bees and other vital pollinators are in decline all over the world, primarily as a result of human activity. It is 'us' that has made life difficult for so many species.

There are several disturbing aspects to the decline in bees and other pollinators. In China, for example, farmers have been forced to hand-pollinate apple and pear trees because bees have been wiped out as a result of the excessive use of pesticides.

In California some 700,000 almond trees require pollination every spring. This task requires the over 40 million bees to be trucked from as far away as Florida to 'pollinate' over a three-week period.

Referred to as 'the industrialisation of pollination,' there are concerns that transporting bees for days across America is a 'stressor' that is weakening their immune system.

But beekeepers all over the world are persisting in the protection and preservation of what have been described as 'tiny miracle workers.'

In Ireland the Native Irish Honey Bee Society (NIHBS) is helping to establish areas of conservation around the country.

David Geoghegan, a second-generation beekeeper from Oughterard, Co. Galway, (see chapter 9) explains: "Not only threatened due to loss of habitat, monoculture, pesticide over-usage and introduced diseases from non-native bee speciceis, now the native Irish black bee has to contend with being 'bred' out of existence."

### KEY FACTS ABOUT BEES

A worker bee will fly the equivalent of one and a half times the circumference of the earth in her 6-8 week life.

◀ *Opposite*: Bee flying back to its hive carrying pollen in a pollen basket.

# PROTECT THE BEES

Everyone can help to protect the honeybee by taking a range of actions including:

## 1
**Grow native wildflowers in your garden or in window boxes**

## 2
**Make sure you have something blooming in every season**

## 3
**Go easy on your use of pesticides, weedkillers and other chemicals**

Beekeeping in Ireland is on the increase and Irish beekeepers are renowed for their willingness to share their knowledge.

But it is from the bees that we can learn most:

- Study what goes on inside the hive to witness collegiality, communication, teamwork and selflessness.

- Watch their navigational skills as they leave the hive and travel up to 5 kilometres for pollen and return.

- Every bee in the hive has a function and the performance of that function is the sole goal.

- The brain of the bee – sized smaller than a sesame seed – has computer-like skills

- … about generosity!

It is appropriate to leave the last words to Dr Thomas Seeley in his book *The Life of Bees*:

> **"More than any other insect, the honey bee has the power to capture our hearts and connect us emotionally with the wonders and mysteries of nature."**

# PICTURE CREDITS

The publisher would like to thank the following for their kind permission to reproduce their photographs and illustrations:

**Joe O'Shaughnessy**, photographs pages: 6, 7, 13, 21, 44, 50, 72, 74-77, 80, 88, 90, 91, 93, 106, 114, 116, 118, 119, 122, 124, 127.

**Valerie O'Sullivan**, photographs pages: 10, 30, 62, 68-69, 98, 100, 103, 106, 108-111.

**An Post**, photographs pages: 132, 134, 135.

**Alexis Sierra**, illustrations page 129.

**Library of Trinity College Dublin.** © The Board of Trinity College Dublin, photography page 24.

**Wikimedia Commons:** Page 16, Gathering Honey, Tomb of Rekhmire © Metropolitan Museum of Art. Page 17, Melittosphex burmensis © Hectarea / CC BY-SA 3.0. Page 20, Stained glass window design of St. Gobnait for Honan Hostel and Chapel, Cork, Ireland © Harry Clarke / Public domain. Collection of the Rakow Research Library, The Corning Museum of Glass, Corning, New York. Page 32 Famine Memorial, Doo Lough, County Mayo © Chris Hood / CC BY (https://creativecommons.org/licenses/by/2.0). Page 56, Filtering of honey © Luc Viatour / https://Lucnix.be. Page 59 (2 photographs) © U.S. Customs and Border Protection / Public domain. Page 64, An overview of the possible causes of the Colony Collapse Disorder phenomenon © Giulia De Rossi, DensityDesign Research Lab. Page 66, Varroa destructor on honeybee host © Courtesy, Erbe, Pooley: USDA, ARS, EMU. Page 67, Honeybee Varroa. © Piscisgate / CC BY-SA. Page 94 (top) Apis mellifera queen © Jonathan Wilkins / CC BY-SA. Page 94 (bottom), Honeycomb of Western honey bees (Apis mellifera) with eggs and larvae © Waugsberg / CC BY-SA. Page 128, The stinger of a black bee © SuperManu / CC BY-SA. Page 138, *Apis mellifera* flying © Muhammad Mahdi Karim / GFDL 1.2.

**Designed by Freepik**, photography page 8 and 41. Illustrations used on pages 14, 20, 22, 28, 34, 42, 48, 54, 60, 70, 78, 86, 96, 104, 112, 120, 130, 136.

**Kat Jayne/Pexels**, photography in this page

# Want to keep reading?

Currach Books has a whole range of books to explore.

As an independent Irish publisher, dedicated to producing quality Irish interest books, we publish a wide variety of titles including history, poetry, biography, photography and lifestyle.

All our books are available through
**www.currachbooks.com**
and you can find us on Twitter, Facebook and Instagram to discover more of our fantastic range of books. You can sign up to our newsletter through the website for the latest news about events, sales and to keep up to date with our new releases.

*currachbooks*    *CurrachBooks*    *currach_books*

CURRACH
BOOKS